LOCAL
VERTICAL

LOCAL VERTICAL

→→ *poems by* ←←

ANNE LINDBERGH

DAVID R. GODINE
BOSTON

First published in 2000 by
David R. Godine, Publisher
Post Office Box 450
Jaffrey, New Hampshire 03452

Copyright © 2000 by Reeve Lindbergh
Foreword © 2000 by Noel Perrin

All rights reserved. No part of this book may be used
or reproduced in any matter whatsoever without written
permission, except in the form of brief citations embodied
in critical articles and reviews.

Library of Congress Cataloging-in-Publication Data
Lindbergh, Anne
Local vertical: poetry / Anne Lindbergh.
p. cm.
ISBN: 1-56792-125-6
I. Title.
PS3562.I4965 L63   2000
811.54—dc21   00-035452

First edition, 2000

This book was printed on acid-free paper.
Printed in the United States of America

Foreword
→→ ←←

The life of Anne Spencer Lindbergh divides rather neatly into four parts, each a little shorter than the one before. The first section lasted for twenty years, from her birth in New York in 1940 until halfway through her sophomore year at Radcliffe in 1960. That year she visited Paris, liked what she saw, and stayed on for fifteen years. She married a Frenchman, lived on the Ile Saint-Louis, bore two children, and began to publish.

Like many in her family, she had been writing since she was a small child, but now, from Paris, she began to send stories to American magazines such as *Vogue* and *Redbook*, and editors snapped them up. She also began sending poems to little magazines in America, and those were accepted, too. Perhaps not snapped up, because poetry editors are generally too glutted with submissions to feel an actual hunger for more. Poets know this, and have developed a thousand strategies for getting attention. Sometimes they seem more businesslike than actual business people, Robert Frost observed in the poem "New Hampshire." They have to be, he explained. "Their wares are so much harder to get rid of." But Anne placed some all the same. She also placed her first book. In 1974, writing as Anne Feydy (Mme. Julien Feydy, if you prefer) she published *Osprey Island*, a novel for children roughly ten to fourteen.

But the second period was fast ending. In 1975 she came back to the United States, and settled in Washington, D.C. Here she stayed for a dozen years.

All of them were productive, though not all of them were happy. The products were of two kinds. She wrote and published six more novels. All were intended for children and adolescents, and all involved some degree of magic. Among the best of them are *The Prisoner of Pineapple Place* and *The Hunky-Dory Dairy*.

She also wrote, and did not publish, several hundred more poems. Many are sad; she was most the poet when she was most unhappy. Of these three hundred or so poems, this small book contains 87. They were chosen by an informal committee consisting of Anne Lindbergh's sister Reeve (herself a writer of some distinction), her daughter Constance, her son Marek, her husband Noel Perrin, and the book's publisher, David Godine. The title was chosen by Anne herself, back in 1982.

Before you go on to the poems, though, I want to say a little about the fourth, last, and briefest period of her life. In 1987, following a divorce, Anne left Washington and moved with her children to a mini-farm in Vermont: eleven acres, with just enough of it pasture to sustain two horses. Here she lived, part-time, until her death in 1993. She wrote little or no poetry in those years from age 47 to death at 53. I make bold to say this was because she was too happy. A few months after moving to Vermont she met another Vermont writer—me—and a few months after that we got married. I want to give a brief picture of our life as a two-writer family.

Anne's study is downstairs; mine is upstairs. Hers contains a large word processor, a laptop, a printer, and a fairly rapid copy machine. Mine contains an electric typewriter (for which I will soon have trouble getting ribbons).

That's up at her house. At my house, 46 miles to the south, her study is an elegant little room built inside one corner of the barn; mine is still upstairs. Hers contains no machinery at all except when she's in residence, and then it has the laptop she brings with her. Mine has an electric typewriter identical to the one I keep at her house, and a rather slow copy machine.

These rooms are emblematic. Though we never had an argument about writing, we had plenty about equipment. Well, discussions really. She thought I was foolish not to use a computer. I'd answer that computers should not be encouraged. There's a real danger, I'd say, that 30 years from now computers will be doing most of the thinking, and the majority of human beings will be disempowered.

"If you had a computer, you could be moving paragraphs around right now," she'd retort, "and that's being *em*powered."

"But I get my paragraphs in the right order to begin with," I'd say smugly.

That's as close to a professional difference as we ever got. Mostly it was pure joy being married to another writer. Why wouldn't it be? The central thing about any marriage is communication. Writers are professional communicators. If words failed us when we talked—and that was rare—one or the other of us wrote a letter. Once we both did, met halfway as we hand-delivered, sat down together and read the two letters. End of fuss.

Any two-writer menage has the resources of language available. But Anne's and my household was especially harmonious, and I think there were three reasons.

The first was very simple. We were not in competition. Anne wrote long, I wrote short. Anne wrote fiction and poetry. I wrote—not fact entirely, but some combination of pieces, casuals, reviews, rural essays, and even the occasional ungainly op-ed.

Of course I admire fiction, and some of Anne's books, like *The Shadow on the Dial*, took my breath away. I just can't write the stuff myself. I've tried. Once I spent a month at the writers' colony called Yaddo. For 27 days I did draft after draft of the first chapter of what was to be a novel set in the small, hate-filled office of a trade magazine. I had plenty of plot, but I could not create one single character. They were just names.

On the 28th morning, I finally got a good idea. I took the whole two-pound mass of drafts, and threw it out. Then I sat down to compose an essay. By that evening I had typed a semi-final version. The piece later appeared in *The New Yorker*.

Anne, on the other hand, could work out whole scenes in her head. She might stock one with five or even ten characters, each distinct. She could get that scene onto a disk with astonishing speed.

But take something easy, like a book review, and she suffered for a week. Once I persuaded her to take on a biography of the Wright brothers. All she had to write was 800 words. First she read the book—twice. Then she composed eight or nine versions of the review, moving paragraphs around like mad. The final two she read aloud to me. I liked them both, despite her obvious reluctance to say anything negative about a book which deserved a few negatives. But she never touched another review. She said writing novels was easier.

I mentioned that Anne read her two final versions to me. I also read my work aloud to her. In fact, I sometimes couldn't make myself wait until an essay was finished. I'd come running downstairs with the first two pages in my hand. Provided she wasn't writing herself, I'd try them out on her. She didn't need to speak. Just from how the two pages sounded as read to her, I knew what worked and what didn't, and could go confidently back upstairs to make changes.

Anne had more self-control. She sometimes waited until a whole book was done before she read it to me. Once, though we normally kept country hours, that meant she read aloud until 3 A.M. Then she was up at seven, moving a few paragraphs.

Need I say it? A fellow writer to whom you're married is the ideal person to read aloud to.

But the best time of all to be married to another writer is when you have to travel. Writing itself is a lonely business (unless you have a wife out in the barn, who will be in for lunch). Going to the Miami Book Fair to sit at a long table with ten other writers and very occasionally autograph a book is even lonelier—unless your wife is beside you, somewhat less occasionally autographing one of hers, and whispering funny remarks in between.

Within a month or two of our marriage, Anne and I turned ourselves into a package deal. If a bookstore invited one of us, it got both. Once in a while, in Vermont or New Hampshire, I'd sell more copies than she did. Anywhere else she outsold me ten to one. All except once. That was at the Cheshire Cat in Washington, her favorite children's bookstore. They naturally didn't carry my books. On our last visit there, the store was jammed—actual lines of children and mothers waiting for an inscription and perhaps a word or two with the author. There the ratio was a hundred to zero.

I didn't mind. I was sitting next to her, feeling useful, opening books to the signing page, so she could concentrate on inscribing and on talking.

About halfway through, a grandmother came up with two curly haired grandsons. They turned to Anne, but the grandmother talked to me.

"You're Noel Perrin, aren't you?" she said. "We used to read you in the *Post*. We were so pleased when you and Anne got married. You're two of our favorite authors, and it felt almost like family. I just wanted to tell you that we moved your books next to hers on the shelf."

Victorian book-collectors sometimes thought it necessary to keep male and female authors separate. I'm glad Anne and I lived when we did.

—Noel Perrin

Local Vertical

"It turns out that you carry with you your own body-oriented world, independent of anything else, in which *up* is over your head, *down* is below your feet, *right* is this way and *left* is that way; and you take this world around with you wherever you go.

This phenomenon had never been apparent on earth, where a man's own local vertical was overridden by his sense of balance."

A House in Space
Henry S.F. Cooper Jr.

March 30

The April wind blows down my street
and the magnolias
would put a fir to shame.
The mockingbird outsings the sparrow.
Neighbors of mine have planted daffodils
to defy the asphalt
with polite rebellion.
It is very soft and pleasant,
nothing to offend the eye.
But all the same I need stone.
Water and stone
and a shore to walk along
alone.

March 31

Certain days I am
sky-giddy, weather-proud
when wind is lavender
and heaven-high.
My feet leave town.
They shuffle through some cloud
and people say
why did she go away
leaving her shoes on the street?
My heart leaves town. I think:
A fine day for gulls!
Suitable weather for crows!
A good wind for swallows!
and where they go I follow
and until evening,
never look down.

March 31

Far be it from me to criticize
but I can't help noticing that you are
upside down
inside out
and crooked.
Your tongue is where your heart should be.
Your ears are where your eyes should be.
Your eyes have gone away
and your feet are everywhere.
You are all wrong.
Far be it from me to offer unsolicited
advice but you might try to
turn around
jump up and down
spin a little.
Then wait very quietly
and hope the pieces settle
where they belong.

March 31

I am no gardener.
The pain of death and birth
is great enough without
the extra weight of flowers.
I only have a garden
because I need a place
to keep the rain.
When I hear the earth
drinking, the drops falling
leaf to leaf there is
a lightening of grief.
I have no love for gardens
but mine and I have made
a pact which we will keep
until one of us should die.

April 3

The west wind flung the ravens at the sky
black on black,
flipped the oak leaves belly up,
flung down the rain
and then blew off again
over the hill and left me
calling, calling
why did you pass me by?
I would follow anywhere
rather than stand here earthbound
with the last drops falling.

April 3

The cardinal
drums his song into the rain
too rapidly and
with a note of panic
like a red heart
beating
as if he only could sustain
his color in this grayness
by repeating
and repeating

April 4

After the rain
the sky shrank into the tighter blue,
the twigs rattled a percussion beat,
the catkins rang like bells.
The day was over-sharpened.
The roofs of the buildings cut the air
and color sliced into color.
I kept my hands in my pockets,
bent my head
not to shred my skin
on the razor edges of sunlight.

April 10

Then unexpectedly the snow was gone
and underneath the earth was bloodless,
winter-numbed, emerging from darkness,
and the sky was pallid
with a moon husk blown into a corner
like a discarded grievance.
The wind died and the day was motionless
save a few crows fleeing lethargy
towards rumors of newer battles.

April 17

Certain trees are naked even
Clothed with leaves.
They have good bones.
They wear the seasons
only for convenience.
Their kind of loveliness transcends
the rules of fashion
and if they wear ivy wound around
the wrist, a bird's nest
in the hair by accident,
it sets a trend.
Given the trouble some trees take
to deck themselves with flowers
it seems hardly fair.

April 17

The only place to be alone
is where you aren't because
nobody looks for you there.
You can walk in total confidence
that you won't meet yourself.
It's worth the trip and heaven knows
it's not the easiest place to reach
Better go before the crowds
discover it and it becomes
Miami Beach.

April 17

then there are days spent
fighting darkness
heavier than sunlight it
sinks to the bottom of the cup
denser than joy it
chokes the breath it
curls up on the ground for
me to stumble over
like death it waits for
me in ordinary places where I
used to be safe it
begins to look at me through
familiar faces that it
borrows without asking and I
fight darkness with darkness and
darkness wins

April 18

Not the first growing when suddenly
the first raw buds appear
after all, barely visible
and life keeps its promise
not a moment too soon—
but the second growing, the unfolding,
is joy. When silence vibrates
with a thousand hands opening,
fingers uncurling green
and green and green.
The song of the thrush is irrelevant,
the apple blossom mere distraction.
Listen for the other bloom—
See the other music!

April 18

Earlier this afternoon
I was standing in a field
barefoot in April
and the sun was hot
and the earth was cold
and the voices of April
sang in my ear.
Why was I hauled in like
a kite at the end of a string
to sit in this dark room
stifled with velvet
for four men in black tails
playing Mozart?
There must be some mistake.
Mozart is where I was,
not here.

April 18

Little plump person in a red hat
I love you
I love your swollen feet
squeezed into your shoes
I love your pearls
and your tight white gloves
and your tight white curls and
I love your eyes that love Mozart
from behind pain. I even
love the smell of your cough drop
but I cannot love
the sound of your fingers
teasing the cellophane.

April 19

I am growing a little tired of pigeons
with their puffy-breasted arrogance.
Tired of pigeons
strutting street-wise, city-proud
and always looking down
and nodding, always nodding.
If it were allowed
pigeons would wear pin striped suits,
tuck the paper under a wing
and hail a cab to show
they have important places to go.
I am growing very tired of pigeons.
Pigeons never sing.
They clear their throats and mumble
at each other, always speeches.
They may have portentous things to say
but I'd rather listen to a sea gull
any day.

April 25

Noah wakes in the dark of night
when the mind is defenseless.
More rain: it's driving everyone
a little mad.
Oh, to have had the sense
to build a bigger ark!
Is he running out of grain?
What happened to the other kangaroo?
There should be two.
What a nuisance to be always
keeping track of pairs.
Can he survive the clutter?
He was unfair to chide his wife
at dinner, but God—
for a place to be alone
if only for an hour!
If he were a sinner
he would be sleeping now,
beneath the flood
but rest is reserved for the wicked.

April 25

Dust falls surreptitiously
like midnight snow.
Weeds grow
in the space of a distraction,
glasses chip, cracks dart across a plate
fast as lizards startled in the sun.
Each thing I see cries out for action
but my heart is aching:
always repairing what is made
and never making.

April 27

Your poem begins with a grain of sand
that chafes the soft beast in the mind
until the mind performs
and smooths the pain with layered ornament:
lustrous perfection of measurable worth.
I covet the round pearl in your hand
but I preferred the grain of sand.

May 1st

Most days come pre-sliced
but sometimes if you're lucky
you get the uncut loaf—
warm and full and fragrant,
all your own.
Think twice before you touch the knife
and mind how you butter your hours!

May 3

I was impatient with the spring.
Green was too much in accord with green—
the beech, the elm, the sweet-gum tree
so much the same
and no depth to the woods at all
until I heard
the distant singing of a bird.
What song will call
out of the closeness of the day
reminding me
that there is still a far-away?

⁂

I dreamed a dream when the sunlight struck the leaf
and something was understood and something learned
but while I dreamed the muffins burned

May 4

Here we go round
binding day to day
with the figures of our dance.
learning not the meaning
but the way.
Here we go round
and weave our circle knowing that inside
somewhere the meaning is implied
in the step, the music or the rhyme—
but there is time to find it.
There is time
so we curtsey and we sway
and we dip and bend.
Why should the music end?
Here we go round and round
the thing we never say.

Ann Arbor, May 7

The sky crouched over the lawn
spitting rain into the shrubbery
and the wind shuddered
and the twigs turned black
and the smell of winter leaves
returned, rank and resentful.
Morning never came
and afternoon was late, arriving
hand in hand with evening
for a quick, dispassionate
glimpse of the day.
You were little comfort—
February in your eye,
March in the set of your jaw,
Saying the garden needed rain.
But did I need to cry?

May 7

gentle tragedy discovered
in the woods in May
feathers on the path—
life is so newly absent
gone perhaps
at the sound of footsteps—
what to say to the child?
the blessing? or the prayer?
the brief assurance of
the scheme of things—
how to explain?
faith is not enough
nor reason—

how to forestall the pain
the rising terror and
the rage that I
(creator, keeper,
guardian of light,
unraveller of wrong and
soother of injustice)
Cannot bring to life
one bird that used to
fly as free as laughter
branch to branch—
nor justify

May 8

the hill lies gentle
under a gentle sky
the sky is feather soft
the saplings feather green
the green is still
with stillness of first spring
the spring wind soft
among the soft grass on
the beast-back of the hill

give me one part water
nine parts sky
color them lavender and
gray of sea-washed stone
and give me stone—
granite shoulders
reaching to the tide
throw in a gull or two
and when you're through
come sit down by my side
for half an hour silently
and then leave me alone

Georgetown, May 12

Suddenly I am annoyed by music—
unmentionable symptom of
what obscure disease?
Perhaps too much a listening inside
for the inner structure,
for the private theme.
Perhaps a wish of weaving
the unruly world into
some harmony—
the tune that can be carried,
the refrain defying
chaos, coming back again
to reassure.
But I have heard nothing,
not even silence
and if this is true—
that there is neither song nor silence—
music will do.

May 11

Shutter all the windows, bar the door—
    Pain is what a house is for.
Close your eyes when other eyes beseech,
    turn away from arms that reach.
There is no commitment without cost—
    nothing is loved but can be lost.
Better not to meet than have to part—
    there is no armor for the heart.
But always light seeps in through cracks, and dust.
    No house is built that you can trust,
So you may wake one day to find you care
    a little too much for a chair.

May 17

my secret friend
the little wind-up man inside
who keeps my legs moving
folds the laundry
combs my hair
looks before I cross the street
busy busy busy
sure he chips a cup or two
cuts my finger with the paring knife
but he has the patience of a saint
he never cries when I cry
I say little man
where's your key your battery
do you need new parts
a drop of oil maybe
please don't leave me
he says lady
don't worry your pretty
head about a thing
just sit back and die.

May 19

She wears her face
in a little patch in front
a busy little patch
two inches wide
pinned down securely
by her nose
I said lady
where's the rest of you?
She said
out shopping

May 20

As I travel
life becomes overpopulated
with impostors of myself.
Each time I return
Where I have been
(and sometimes where I never was)
one of them is there
daring me to prove her false.
My old friends say
(and sometimes new)
"Someone you have to meet—
I know you'll get on fine—
she and you are just alike!"
What's the use of denying?
They laugh in my face
so I agree
to wear her skin, her voice,
her threadbare thoughts
but when I leave
I make sure she doesn't
follow me.
The more old selves that you discard
the lonelier you are.

May 20

I contrived a poem for you
that was more beautiful than true
about a morning in the wood
when all the world was pure and good.
I made the stream we walked along
accompany our steps with song.
For you I forced an apple tree
to blossom into poetry.
In secret, while you praise and quote
I now compose my antidote:
    poison ivy
    broken bottles in the stream
    mosquitoes
    and the dead raccoon
    unmentionable souvenirs
    of sex discarded
    on the path
    and mud
    and bottle caps
    and beer.
When you return to the world of men
come walk in the wood with me again.

May 21

I prefer weeds in cities.
Flowers are nothing but veneer
to flatter the foolish
into thinking life is here.
But when I see dandelions
where streets were respectable before,
and liverwort around the drain,
and beggar's-ticks and creeping buttercup
weaving tangled scandal at my door
and toadstools forcing through the asphalt
after rain, and honeysuckle
teasing the pampered rose
and puffballs on the lawn
where no high-minded flower grows,
and poison sumac, nettles, jimson weed,
I am reassured
and breathe more easily
knowing that chaos has endured,
the bowels of the city having failed
to digest the seed.

May 23

A discretion of finches
A corruption of grackles
An accusation of jays
A presumption of pigeons
An aggravation of crows
An apparition of cardinals
A vexation of sparrows
A consolation of doves
My garden is the Marriott Hotel
Overbooked with conventions
I feel shy in the corner of the elevator
The only one not wearing a name tag:
    Glad to meet you!
    I'm a bird.

My children only pretend
to leave the house
they can't fool me
after I shut the door on them
I find them hiding
in their pockets

May 26

Why are my senses
sequestrated like a
formal fountain jetting sprays
this way and that,
calculated architecture:
touching, hearing, taste
all different,
sight and scent apart
even if parallel,
thought independent
and meanwhile my body
(unanthenticated othersense)
slung like a bag
from mind. Will I
be permanently shattered,
parlor puzzle never
to be solved or
should I be content
to be a question?

May 28

for their anniversary
in almost June
they hired a summer night
a cosmetician came to their own home
to touch up their expression of delight
they were allowed to rent the moon
by special dispensation
the illumination lasted until dawn
at astronomical expense
and they strolled arm in arm
about the lawn admiring
the annual reconfirmation
of their elegance
(the best self-offense
is a good self-defense)

May 30

Heat made the honeysuckle
twirl in giddy tendrils,
made two butterflies
stagger through the dappled light,
made the white-throated sparrow
a little mad with repetition:
"Sweet—
  ripe—
  strawberry strawberry strawberry!"
When the sky is heavy
the weak are permitted to rebel.

Let's not explore—
the illusory is best.
I have already guessed
there is a house
behind those trees
and someone lives inside.
under the water noise
I can't quite hide
the sound of a highway
further down the stream.
Let's not explore—
let's dream.

June 2

This morning seven saplings
were delivered to my street.
They lie waiting
sprawled like lanky adolescents,
their blowsy summer leaves
strewn recklessly on the cement
a little limp,
their roots still bound
in swollen sacking
next to seven plots
of newly turned-up earth.
I look more closely: maples.
Tomorrow they will be erect,
roots exploring the plumbing,
leaves searching for a sky.
I wish they could stay
forever lying down.
There is too much vertical
already in this town.

June 7

I am a tree
rooted stubbornly,
clutching a fistful
of quiet, dark things
underground.
I am a boulder
nested in the earth,
my permanence
confirmed by lichen.
I do not migrate.
You think I travel
everywhere with you.
I know:
I never go.

June 11

Whoever stole my cloak of darkness
don't bring it back
I don't need it any more
I am out of mourning
(in any case
I never knew for whom
or what I mourned)
Whoever stole my cloak of darkness
how can I reward you—
a golden ducat?
a bowl of porridge at the door?
whoever stole my cloak
wear it in light
it has served
its other purpose

June 22

Last night a foreign thing
strayed into town,
hinting of other places.
I breathed what could have been
the smell of new-mown grass;
in a lull of traffic
I almost heard a sea gull call;
a wave approached
and nearly struck the shore.
How was this wildness
wooed out of darkness
to beat against the city
like a blinded moth?

Maine—June 30

Kennebunkport, Biddeford—
driving north
the highway sheds its terror
and becomes a song
with the old refrain of names
pulling me along.
Falmouth, Freeport, Bath—
the migratory path
going with the gulls
toward the white-throated sparrow
and a field of Queen Anne's lace
and yarrow.

July 1

I woke to a construction paper day
the sky was flat and uniform
the grass uncompromising green
and in between no shadow
nothing to be
but a paper figure under a paper tree
nothing to do
but cut out a yellow paper sun
and paste it on the blue

North Haven, July 2

come with me early to the shore
down the unmown path
beneath the fir
where the goldfinch dances
to the sparrow's song
we won't be long
only a moment to explore
this summer's disposition
only the time to run
the cove's length at the tide line
where the kelp is drying
and the driftwood bone
bleached by the winter sun
and hear once more
the wave ring hollow on the stone
and the sea birds crying

July 4

The grasshopper discards
his skin repeatedly.
Why can't I also shed
the old form and again
begin? The hermit crab
deserts his outgrown shell
and finds another—
Why not I as well?
Even serpents moult.
I alone cannot revolt,
have no room to unfold
the newer self imprisoned
in the old.

July 4

I was happy with the names of things
until a child told me
kelp was dragon skin,
the petal of the beach rose—
poison tongue,
the daisy—fried egg flower,
and on the shore among the stones
were tiger bones.
Then I grew wild with naming-power
and was not satisfied
until each once-familiar thing
revealed the secret self
it hid inside.

July 6

Where is my adolescent rage
of the day the field was mown—
the tractor straining to efface
black-eyed Susan,
Queen Anne's lace,
and nothing left but lawn?
Is it so adult and wise
to savor the impending loss,
love the meadow for the mowing,
prize it all the more
for knowing
by night it will be gone?

July 7

There is an awesome arrogance
to ugly things—
they become sacred.
Why do I rearrange
the jar of roses
or the cushions on a chair
but would not dare to change
the plastic lampshade,
take it on myself
to remove the leering shepherdesses
from the shelf?

July 19

the salt fog breathes over the meadow
quiet as a windless tide—
sifts through the round rocks,
the bay bush, the briar rose,
softens the jagged line of fir
while the moaning horn uncurls along the shore
making us more island than we were

July 22

What did I leave behind, up the white wake?
    only what I wanted most to take—
    the breath of bay and beach-plum rose
    above the tide line where the wild pea grows
    and seaweed crusted on the beach
    and the wide-elbowed cormorants
    that reach their wings to dry
    out on the dark rock, over the water
    and the cry of gull, the echo of the loon
    and the sodden salt smell
    rising from warm stone at noon
    and the frail-fingered hermit crab
    curled in his shell—
What did I leave behind up the white wake?
only what I wanted most to take—

August 16

The only inland sin is tidelessness—
water and wind are there
but not the salt smell
when the water slips back
leaving the mud flats bare
nor the high tremor of the wind
when the wave swells against the shore
like a great beast breathing.
Inland hours
march to the rhythm of the sun
through night and noon
but here they dance
to the slow rotation of the moon.

September 23

And overnight September came
with an upward gust of joy,
carrying leaves all the way
to the white day-moon—
Come too! Come too!
Not often is the passage open
clear through.

September 27

When the wind takes possession
I surrender easily
my earthly ways
and all the hoarded profit
of repeated days.
When the wind calls, I follow—
why should I alone
remain, by breath and blood
rooted to stone?

October 15

as uniform excuses death
the (boy in khaki is
neither himself nor you)
violinist in black tails
urbanely wounds
the soul and we (applaud
but let neither sinner
venture on the stage
barefooted lest we)
find ourselves likewise naked

October 20

Arrows and crossways,
interdictions, passages
are balm for those of us
who lose connection
between place and soul.
As clocks connive a whole
when time is structureless,
so the sign atones
for lack of reason,
spelling the unalterable way
across the vacant day.
During the joyless season
habits are my bones.

November 12, Connecticut

at last the trees
strip to the bare bone
discarding the leaf
the summer sheen
the scarlet twist of ivy,
the last compromise.
now for the business
of winter,
the fulfillment
of the one true pact
with sky—
I too have bones
I will not forget my bones

November 19, Georgetown

This November morning is
gray only to the outward eye,
but watch!
Strip back the sky!
Beyond is my blood-red scream.
Yes, it left me—
escaped through a momentary stillness.
Why should it stay inside
when the inner voice is silent
and the inner space
too small to hide?

January 1983, Florida

more beautiful
is not the flawless day
the palm retaining every frond
unyielding green
imprinted on pure blue
each line a boundary
between two facts
each fact defined—
    but troubled mornings
    when horizon is
    both sea and sky
    and the heron wavers
    double-stemmed
    above his image

January

Until the farthest reach of land
the towers stand
eyeless at the flattened sea
before the final boundary
where old men walking on the sand
patrol the edge
of no man's land.
They came this far
to throw a cantilever to a star
but they have already built
too many bridges.
Now they must learn
to burn.

June 9

rolling days
make hoops
of themselves
each tail caught
in the teeth
of morning
do they roll
forward or
are they only
rocking
surely there is
substance here
within
the pattern but
I thrust
my heart through
the hoop and
feel
nothing

June 12

I know the tree will die.
There, where its branches
give dimension to the sky,
will be untempered blue
in a tree's death—
say a hundred years.
And where I move across the field
will be neither man nor field
in a man's death—
which may well be now.
Yet all this, in strong moments,
is serenity
for why am I flesh if not
to scorn such matters temporarily?
Only say, for the soul's sake,
that the song will stay
as it has before
and after all that I have known
and each illusion, every dream,
and will sustain
the unrelenting mockery
of its refrain.

November 1

The meaning of life,
like the cat,
has its haunts and habits:
here at daybreak,
there at dusk,
even its mysteries
conducted tidily
until one morning
poof—it's gone!
Leaving a shadow
to brush against
the back of your mind
asking to be let in
or out.

November 17

(Reeve)

now is the time to go—
when the leaf goes,
when the sky is cracked open
for the wind to slip through,
when still water deepens
to a darker dimension.
One sign only,
a single invitation—
now is the time to go.

December 13

(From the Dentist's Chair)

In offices across the way
women shuffle papers,
talk, type, turn, exit and enter
through open doorways.
They have nothing to hide.
Yet by something in the set of their shoulders
I know they know:
through cracks in the venetian blinds
where pain slivers into sunlit parallels
hungrily I sap the ease
from their untroubled motions.

April 18

(Riddle)

I reach to you under the April tree
and again
I stand there watching me,
and a third more distant still
regrets plurality.
Of so many voices which one lies?
What act is true
if every act is seen through other eyes?
Which touch is real and which is art?
How many-layered is the heart?

November 13

(How to Make Space Around You)

Pick a crowd you would like to thin,
stretch out your arms
and spin.

In moments of extreme despair,
crouch and gradually rise
to clear a column in the air.

If the crowd is slow in thinning,
keep spinning.

January 19, 1985

(Development)

After the tree is gone,
when the meadow is no longer there
and walls of stone have claimed
another square of sky
is when the fiercest life begins for me.
Each leaf, and branch, and hidden nest
and all the grasses too, have come
to rest here, in my eye alone.
I cannot talk to you. My every breath
must sing to warm them from their death.

March 20

Hide your secrets where they are
among their kind.
No one will find the flower
among a hundred others in a field—
or, to keep a star,
choose any constellation, slip it inside:
nowhere could it be
more carefully concealed.
And if you must weep,
weep outside in the rain.
Who is to know
which drops are merely weather,
which drops pain?

April 15, East Bay

(Before the Fog Lifts)

I do not care to know
more than the swan's slow, widening ripple
on the lake,
more than the trace of gulls' wings
in the sky.
I will not wait to see
what is beyond this tentative,
accommodating gray.
The line where air and water meet
is in the inner eye.

April 15, East Bay

(Mallards)

See his green-glossed neck,
white-feathered kerchief tucked into his plumage,
while she wears hues of gray.
How gaudily he promenades beside the water!
He has the upper hand.
While she—she waddles, frankly,
and complains: 'Too Far! Too soon!'
and 'Didn't I tell you so?'
nursing her fledgling past
when she was the drake's daughter.
The two of them leave
wedge-shaped footprints in the sand.

April 16, in flight

These western roads cut straight through,
make free of the earth
as birds do of the sky.
I am like New England roads—
circumventing here a feeling,
there a barn,
as I pass by.

May 2

Little Anne is curled under a stone.
Leave her alone.
A single step outside and who is to know
where she might not go?
She might fly clear up to the moon
and hide, and then slip down,
spread out in a thousand dust motes
under the sun, at noon.
She might simply walk away
and not come back at the end of the day.
Little Anne is curled under a stone.
Leave her alone.

May 10, 1985

    (Snow White: The King's First Wife)

Already she was numb, resigned to life:
winter, boredom, the long days
at the window, in the raw air, stitching
work a servant could do just as well,
and never any praise.
There was no pleasing the king,
barren as she was—an unwomanly condition.
No wonder it vexed her
that the needle pierced her thumb.
It was the final straw.
In despair she called out for a daughter.
When all else fails,
pain justifies itself by repetition.

III.

(Unspeakable)

No silliness exceeds
the silliness of flesh:
bones and blemishes,
the care-worn and the scarred,
every angle an embarrassment,
every softness marred,
each fault, once skillfully disguised,
so hard to face—
inanity and love so hard to reconcile.
Yet we embrace,
accommodate our two absurdities
and in our braver moments
even smile.

June 12, Darien

There is a wall around me
of your faces—
an impenetrable wall.
I can't feel my way through.
I can't even see them all,
only traces.
Will you hear me if I shout?
Where do I batter with my fists?
Where do I gnaw
with my pale, sharp teeth?
But you—you will not admit
the wall exists.
Inward is the only way out.

June 20, North Haven

This much is sure—
that I am here again
at the morning window in another year
as are the wings, the birdsong
and the line of firs against the sky,
the line of winter tides along the beach
and streaks of calm smoothing the ruffled bay.
The things that change the least
are those that never are the same
but are always there.
Endure, return, endure—
and do not compare.

June 21

She has taken to wandering again,
the crazy lady.
See her go—alone, the first to trespass
on the morning quiet
and never a soul goes with her,
never a friend.
Oh, the days, the years she has been wandering—
time out of mind—
and to what end when we all know
if there were anything to find
she would pass by it?

July 6

This year the sparrow's song
is sharp as the meadow grass
 that cuts my hand
when I reach to pull a strand.
This year the tree-line tears the sky
and shards of sunlight fall
to cut my feet when I pass by.
Now the salt air burns my face
and the salt wave chastens
where it used to soothe.
All the comfort of this place
hastens to wound, and I know why.
How dare I come back asking
just because once it gave?

July 23

(Old Maid)

She gave.
There wasn't an item she would save.
We said, it's as if giving
were her only way to go on living.
We said she had a heart of gold
but found her troublesome.
Everyday she'd come around our door
with something more,
and her gifts were so bewildering:
old bits of foil, and salvaged lengths of string.
We begged her to stay and have a cup of tea
but wished she'd go away.
Not heart of gold, we knew—
heartache.
Sometimes to give
is the only way to take

                    (only a ditty,
                    sitting too pretty:
                    When you feel shitty
                    it's hard to be witty.)

July 26

When he was there she put away the mirrors.
Not from shame of vanity—
because her image in his eyes
was self enough to see.
How could she think that image was reflection?
To keep her self inside another
was defection.

July 27

Dawn was fresher than ever
after the gale,
as though she had never been battered.
The wind could tear up every fir tree on the island
for all it mattered to her;
she was still there—
triumphant, though a little pale.
How long will she be content
to stay untroubled, safe and warm before she needs to
prove she's there
against another storm?

October 11, Georgetown

(Just To Put It On Record)

having loved you for a year of seasons
I can now truthfully say
wherever you are
here where I am the world has not changed so very much
since you went away

I understand
it is a time-worn joke
administered in the form of a slap in the face
that the leaves of the sumac will turn red
and the leaves of the tulip tree yellow whether or not
we are together in this place

and whether or not you choose to come back or
pains of pains
turn a second time and go
there will be another winter
with a fair chance of snow

October 13

Every woman is an island:
an upheaval
connected to other islands by the roots
deep down, under the flood,
surrounded by a sea of blood.

Ships pass by us,
signal, or anchor,
land and plunder,
shrink into the horizon
or, in a gale, go under.

We remain
(a geographical irritation
that will, in the course of time, erode)
some to be circumvented,
some exploited,
and a few, volcanic,
to explode.

January 8, 1986

Utter misery
for a short time is release.
The thread that binds you to belief
gives way. One day you find
that you no longer feel, no longer care.
You are so far removed
that after all perhaps there was no pain,
you never loved, and memory
becomes so old that also memory
was never real. For a short time
you bless the flame that cannot burn
until you learn how cold it is out there,
how very cold.

November 1987, Vermont

Post Mortem

Would you do it again if I could make you see
    the banality?
People who could no more catch you than the wind
    define you now
with words that print across the white page of your
                                 absence
Dead words:
I hold my heart to them and feel no breath.
Would you do it again if I told you yes
There is an afterlife. I
    am living it.
This morning for instance the last apples on the tree
glowed in the first frost
like lesser moons against the early sky.
    But you!
This is the first day of the rest of your death.

LOCAL VERTICAL

was set in a digitized version of Fournier, a typeface originated by Pierre Simon Fournier *fils* (1712-1768). Coming from a family of typefounders, Fournier was an extraordinarily prolific designer both of typefaces and of typographic ornaments. He was the author of the celebrated *Manuel typographique* (1764-1766). In addition, he was the first to attempt to work out the point system standardizing type measurement, a system that is still in use internationally.

Many aspects of Fournier's personality and period are captured in this typeface, which balances elegance with great legibility.

The book was designed by Dean Bornstein.
The photographs are by Sally Stone Halvorson.